Cowboys

© Aladdin Books Ltd 1995

Designed and produced by
Aladdin Books Ltd
28 Percy Street
London W1P 9FF

First published in 1995 in the United States by
Copper Beech Books, an imprint of
The Millbrook Press
2 Old New Milford Road
Brookfield, Connecticut 06804

Design
David West Children's
Book Design

Designer
Flick Killerby

Editor
Jim Pipe

Picture Research
Brooks Krikler Picture Research

Illustrators
McRae Books, Italy

Library of Congress Cataloging-in-Publication Data
Ross, Stewart.
Cowboys: a journey down the long, lonely cattle
trail in search of the hard-riding, gun-slinging
cowhands of the Old West / Stewart Ross.
p. cm. – (Fact or fiction)
Includes index.
ISBN 1-56294-618-8 (lib.bdg.)
1-56294-636-6 (pbk.)
1. Cowboys – West (U.S.) – Juvenile literature.
2. Frontier and pioneer life – West (U.S.) – Juvenile literature.
3. West (U.S.) – History – Juvenile literature. I. Title.
II. Series: Ross, Stewart. Fact or Fiction.
F596.R825 1995   94-43658
978'.02–dc20   CIP AC

FACT or FICTION:

Cowboys

Written by *Stewart Ross*
Illustrated by *McRae Books, Italy*

COPPER BEECH BOOKS
BROOKFIELD, CONNECTICUT

CONTENTS

INTRODUCTION

Switch on the TV. Flick through the channels. Somewhere, on one of the stations, there will probably be a Western. We recognize the style at once. First, there are the cowboys – tough men on beautiful horses charging about the wild, open country of the American West. The townships of wooden houses and saloons are laid out around a dusty main street. There are stagecoaches, card games, slugs of whiskey, Indians, beautiful women in long dresses and, always, the gunfight.

The cowboy is one of the movie's finest creations. But isn't it odd that, despite the name "cowboy" we don't often see any cows? And why do we call the stars cow*boys* when they are grown men?

The truth is that the heroic cowboys of Westerns are the invention of movie makers. The historical cowboy was a cattle drover. He spent most of his time in the saddle of a small, mangy horse, driving cattle across vast empty spaces. He was poorly paid and, if he got into a fight, slow on the draw. Indians were more likely to be his friends than enemies. In fact, many cowboys were Indians.

Read on. Enter the tough, no-nonsense world of the true cowboy. It has no white stallions and few young ladies in distress. But it is hard, dangerous and, above all, real.

GOING WEST

European settlers arrived in North America in the early 17th century. For over a hundred years they remained largely on the Atlantic seaboard, but by the beginning of the 19th century, the United States was on the move, heading west. By 1820 the frontier was across the Mississippi. Texas was annexed twenty-five years later and by 1853, apart from Alaska, the frontiers of the United States were as they stand today.

Two events followed this expansion. One was the migration of thousands of Americans to start new lives on the Great Plains and beyond. The other was the Civil War (1861–65). The era of the cowboy was about to begin.

STEER ROPERS. One of the biggest differences between screen cowboys and real ones is racial. Movie cowboys are generally white and English-speaking. Many real cowboys were non-white, and the working language of nearly all cowboys was Spanish.

One in seven cowboys was an African American, including two of the most skilled and famous, Nat Love (*above left*) and John Ware. There were also many Native American and Mexican cowboys. But the movie makers had different ideas. When cowboys passed through the filter of Hollywood, only the white ones were left (*above right*), thus creating one of the most powerful myths of modern culture.

Wagon trains were the final phase of westward expansion. First came the explorers and trappers, then the cattlemen, and finally farmers and their families in the long trains of wagons. The three great trail routes ran west from St. Louis and Natchez on the Mississippi, and Fort Smith on the Arkansas River.

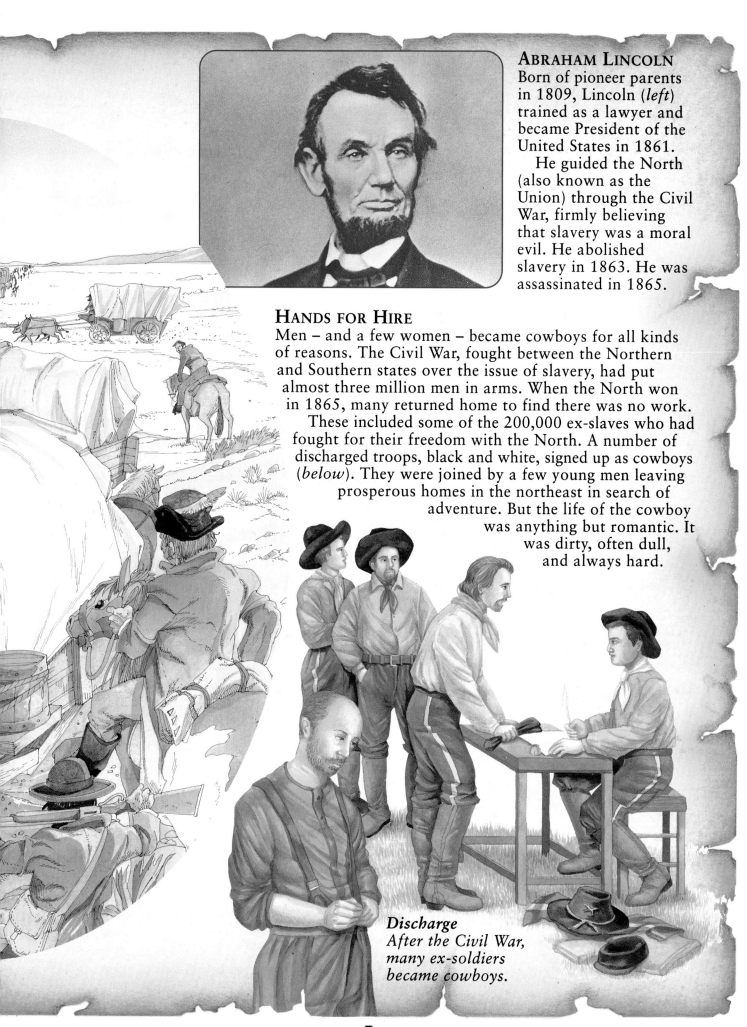

ABRAHAM LINCOLN

Born of pioneer parents in 1809, Lincoln (*left*) trained as a lawyer and became President of the United States in 1861.

He guided the North (also known as the Union) through the Civil War, firmly believing that slavery was a moral evil. He abolished slavery in 1863. He was assassinated in 1865.

HANDS FOR HIRE

Men – and a few women – became cowboys for all kinds of reasons. The Civil War, fought between the Northern and Southern states over the issue of slavery, had put almost three million men in arms. When the North won in 1865, many returned home to find there was no work.

These included some of the 200,000 ex-slaves who had fought for their freedom with the North. A number of discharged troops, black and white, signed up as cowboys (*below*). They were joined by a few young men leaving prosperous homes in the northeast in search of adventure. But the life of the cowboy was anything but romantic. It was dirty, often dull, and always hard.

Discharge
After the Civil War, many ex-soldiers became cowboys.

CATTLE KINGDOM

The Great Plains of Midwest America stretch from Texas to the Canadian border and from Kansas to the Rockies. In the early 19th century the Plains were a sea of long, nourishing buffalo grass. Cattle had been raised here for years, producing meat, hides, horn, and fat. The business was small-scale and local. The Civil War changed all that. Beef was sold to the soldiers, and they grew to like it. So did the city dwellers further east, previously pork eaters. During the war the Plains cattle went unattended, thriving and multiplying. By 1865 there were five million beasts roaming free on the Plains. Businessmen found that an animal worth a few dollars in Texas was now worth up to fifty in the north.

The problem of getting the cattle to the rail stations hundreds of miles away was solved by the "long drive," rounding up herds of cattle and driving them slowly north, fattening them up on the grass as they went (see map, *below*). And who managed the trail? The cowboy.

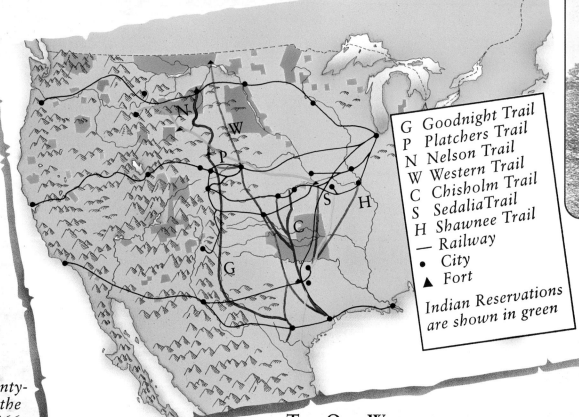

G Goodnight Trail
P Platchers Trail
N Nelson Trail
W Western Trail
C Chisholm Trail
S SedaliaTrail
H Shawnee Trail
— Railway
• City
▲ Fort

Indian Reservations are shown in green

Cattle Kingdom
During the brief twenty-year era of the cowboy (1866–1886), the Great Plains were a "Cattle Kingdom." The "kings" were not the cowboys, but the powerful businessmen who funded the cattle trade and reaped huge profits.

THE OLD WEST

Before the settlement of the West Coast, the Great Plains were the American West. In time the states of the Old West, such as Kansas (in 1861) and Nebraska (in 1867), entered the Union (the President's flag is *top of page*).

REMEMBER THE ALAMO!

Texas, the original home of the cowboy, was for a long time disputed between the United States and Mexico. Thousands of Americans arrived there in the early 19th century, and relations between the settlers and the Mexican government became strained.

War broke out in 1835. The Mexican general, Santa Anna, invaded Texas with an army of 7,000 men. In his path stood the fortified mission of the Alamo, manned by some 220 Texans. This garrison was wiped out, but their heroic stand (later made into a film, *right*) inspired the Texans to defeat Santa Anna eventually. Texas became independent in 1836, and joined the Union eight years later.

CATTLEMEN

The word "cowboy" was coined in Ireland over a thousand years ago. It means a hired rider who looks after cattle. In the Revolutionary War (1775–83) it was used as a term of abuse for farmers who sided with the British. Mexican cowboys were known by the Spanish word *vaqueros*. Texan cowboys used this word, but pronounced it "buckaroo!"

Rough and Ready
Frontier towns (above), *often no more than tents, were where the long trail ended. Once the cattle were sold, cowboys headed for the bathhouse and saloon!*

THE "LONG DRIVE"

Before the long drive began, cattle were rounded up into herds of up to 5,000 three- and four-year-old steers. This might take many days and kept the cowboys in the saddle from dawn to dusk. When the herd was assembled and the strays, called "mavericks," branded (*below*), it moved off north, covering about 15 miles (25 km) a day. By the 1870s the trails were well-worn tracks up to 750 miles (1,200 km) long and 1,300 feet (400 m) wide, stretching over the prairie like dusty highways.

Cowboys liked routes that kept away from hills and woods (the easy places for rustlers and coyotes to attack). At popular destinations, such as Abilene and Dodge City, the cattle were sold and herded into wagons for transport to the slaughterhouse.

CATTLE BARONS

A few men made huge fortunes from the cattle trade. These were the cattle barons who came to control the whole operation, from roundup to slaughter and distribution.

One of the first barons was Philip Armour, who sold beef to soldiers in the Civil War. In time men like Charles Goodnight acquired huge ranches, known as "cattle empires." He alone owned and leased over 1.25 million acres (0.5 million hectares) of Texas land. By 1885, almost 50 per cent of all U.S. land was used for cattle ranching.

remuda

ON THE TRAIL

The formation of a herd on the move was carefully arranged. The trail boss led the way, followed by the other cowboys in pairs. First came the point riders, then the swing and flank men. The drag riders followed behind in a cloud of dust! Spare horses were gathered in a *remuda* and watched by the wrangler.

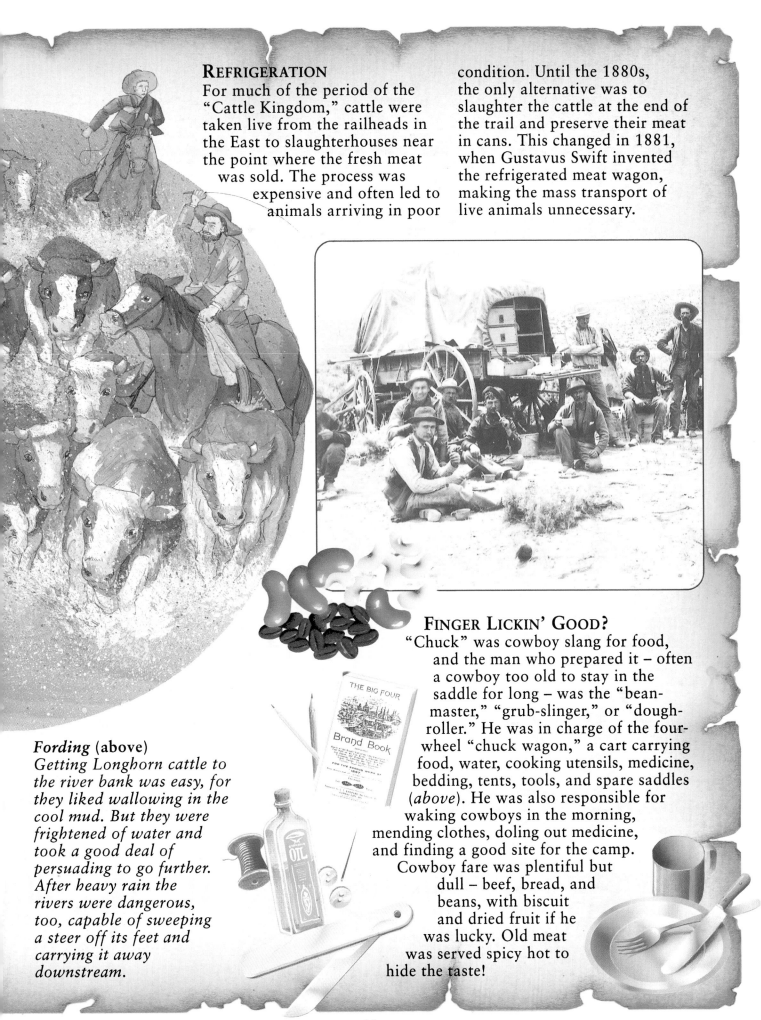

REFRIGERATION

For much of the period of the "Cattle Kingdom," cattle were taken live from the railheads in the East to slaughterhouses near the point where the fresh meat was sold. The process was expensive and often led to animals arriving in poor condition. Until the 1880s, the only alternative was to slaughter the cattle at the end of the trail and preserve their meat in cans. This changed in 1881, when Gustavus Swift invented the refrigerated meat wagon, making the mass transport of live animals unnecessary.

Fording (above)
Getting Longhorn cattle to the river bank was easy, for they liked wallowing in the cool mud. But they were frightened of water and took a good deal of persuading to go further. After heavy rain the rivers were dangerous, too, capable of sweeping a steer off its feet and carrying it away downstream.

FINGER LICKIN' GOOD?

"Chuck" was cowboy slang for food, and the man who prepared it – often a cowboy too old to stay in the saddle for long – was the "bean-master," "grub-slinger," or "dough-roller." He was in charge of the four-wheel "chuck wagon," a cart carrying food, water, cooking utensils, medicine, bedding, tents, tools, and spare saddles (*above*). He was also responsible for waking cowboys in the morning, mending clothes, doling out medicine, and finding a good site for the camp. Cowboy fare was plentiful but dull – beef, bread, and beans, with biscuit and dried fruit if he was lucky. Old meat was served spicy hot to hide the taste!

THE COWBOY AND HIS HORSE

The one thing the real and fictional cowboy have in common is the horse. But even here there is a difference. Film cowboys ride huge animals that never seem to tire. Real cowboys preferred small horses, often ponies, and rarely rode the same one all day.

By 1800 there were two million wild horses, known as mustangs or broncos, roaming the Plains. When tamed, these animals made excellent work horses. Breaking in was the job of the roving bronco-buster, who rode a bronco until it was too exhausted to try to throw him. It was then ready to be trained.

The best horses for roundup work were quarter horses – small, nimble animals capable of great speed over short distances. They were the best cutting horses, used by cowboys to separate unbranded calves from their mothers. They were trained to respond to every movement of the rider. A horse was an expensive piece of equipment and few cowboys owned their own. A single horse was little use anyway – a cowboy changed mounts as often as six times a day.

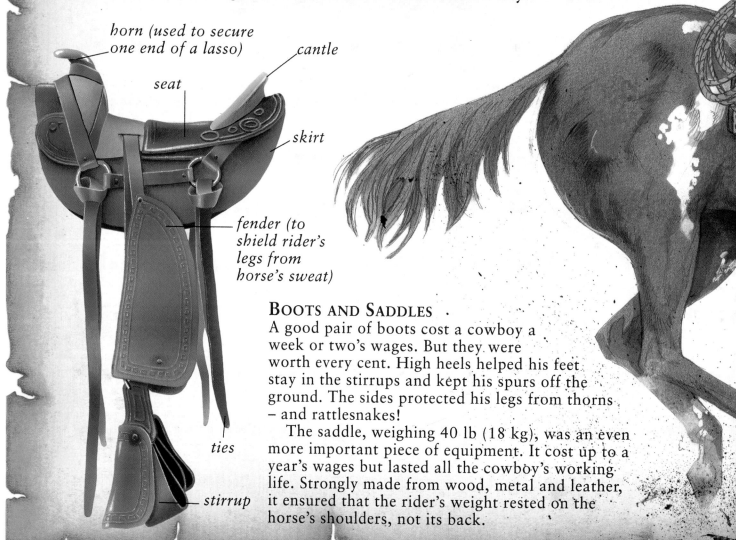

horn (used to secure one end of a lasso)

cantle

seat

skirt

fender (to shield rider's legs from horse's sweat)

ties

stirrup

BOOTS AND SADDLES

A good pair of boots cost a cowboy a week or two's wages. But they were worth every cent. High heels helped his feet stay in the stirrups and kept his spurs off the ground. The sides protected his legs from thorns – and rattlesnakes!

The saddle, weighing 40 lb (18 kg), was an even more important piece of equipment. It cost up to a year's wages but lasted all the cowboy's working life. Strongly made from wood, metal and leather, it ensured that the rider's weight rested on the horse's shoulders, not its back.

The neckerchief had a hundred and one uses. It protected the neck from the sun and made a face mask, bandage, filter, and handkerchief.

The cowboy hat was made from felt, and highly practical. As well as keeping off the sun and rain, it also served as a pail and a fan.

Looking the part. A cowboy's clothes were comfortable but tough. On the trail he probably wore the same shirt and pants every day. At the end of the trail, he threw away his old, worn-out clothes and bought new ones. Only then did he briefly resemble the spick and span movie cowboy (*below*).

Spurs, worn on the heel and used to goad a horse's flank, look cruel (left). In fact, they were used very carefully – spur marks on a horse were a sign of poor horsemanship.

PANTS AND CHAPS

Except in the hottest weather, cowboys wore one-piece underwear known as long johns (*right*). Over this they wore a collarless shirt and, originally, baggy, woolen pants. These were warm, but not very strong. Later they changed to canvas or denim jeans. When in the saddle they wore leather chaps over their pants for warmth and protection. In the coldest weather they wore "hair pants" – hide chaps with the animal's hair or wool left on (the cowboy on page 35 is wearing some).

"BEEVES!"

Like the horse, cattle came into the United States with the Spanish in the 16th century. Three breeds were introduced, the Berrenda, the Retino, and the valuable black bulls, known as Granado Prietos. The last were highly prized and rarely escaped. But the other two breeds were soon roaming wild on the Plains, where they bred to create the famous Longhorns. These were tough, lean-bodied cattle, known as "beeves" by the cowboys. They thrived in very harsh conditions, surviving on only water and grass and keeping marauding wolves and cougars at bay with their ferocious horns. But they were not ideal beef cattle.

Ill-tempered and unpredictable, their massive horns – sometimes measuring over 6 ft (2 m) from tip to tip – made them dangerous to handle. They were also slow to mature and provided poor quality meat. In time, therefore, they were cross-bred with fatter, more docile breeds from Europe.

THE END OF THE LONGHORN

Even while the wild Plains cattle were being rounded up and herded north to the railheads, ranchers were beginning to think toward the future.

The Longhorn was too lean and bad-tempered. Also, its ability to survive on a meager diet became less useful as the expansion of arable farming into the West created a plentiful supply of hay. By the 1870s, cattlemen were experimenting with new breeds, imported from Britain.

The best results were achieved by breeding Hereford bulls with a Longhorn cow. This created calves that were hardy, heavy, and even-tempered. By the 1890s, the once famous Longhorn was a rarity.

New Breeds
The most popular breeds brought from England to replace the Longhorn were the Hereford, a red cow with a white blaze on its face, and the Aberdeen Angus.

Stampede!
Cowboys feared nothing more than a stampede. "Spooked" by a loud noise, the herd suddenly went out of control, charging across the prairie (above).

Longhorn

Shorthorn

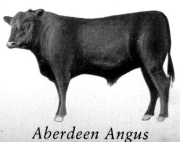

Aberdeen Angus

Hereford

BRANDING

A brand was an owner's mark burned with a hot iron onto an animal's hide. As there were hundreds of brands (*right*), the trail boss carried a book listing all known brands.

Branding was a highly skilled operation. It took place after the roundup, when all recently born calves were separated from their mothers. First, a mounted cowboy lassoed the calf. Then two flankers tipped it onto its side and held it fast while the brander applied the red-hot branding iron (*below*). Other men kept the angry mother at bay as she tried to rescue her calf.

Ropes
A cowboy's rope, known as a lariat or lasso, was originally made from cowhide or twisted grass. By the end of the 1890s hemp was the most popular material, as it allowed longer ropes to be used.

A full lariat, about 60 ft (18 m) long, was made by braiding together a number of shorter ropes.

Famous brands

THE BUFFALO

The North American bison, more commonly known as the buffalo, was one of the natural wonders discovered by the Spanish in the New World. They found a truly majestic creature, standing over 4.5 feet (1.5 m) high and weighing almost a ton when fully grown, with a mane like a lion and a hump like a camel.

Apart from the look of the creature, it was the number of buffalo that most impressed the first explorers and hunters. It is estimated that before the westward expansion of the United States, between 50 and 150 million buffalo roamed the Great Plains, sometimes in herds of 20,000 or more. Until the middle of the 19th century, the buffalo population was stable. Although a few were killed by the Native Americans and by white hunters, the great majority lived as they had always done, grazing the broad grasslands.

However, buffalo grass was also the staple diet of the Longhorn. Within a few decades, the preserve of the bison had become that of the cattle rancher and farmer, and the native species had been hunted almost to the point of extinction.

SLAUGHTER

The hunting of the North American buffalo (*above*) was one of America's most shameful acts of wanton destruction. By 1900, the official census counted just 541 animals left alive on the Plains.

The massacre began as a quest for food to supply the railway laborers and ranchers working their way across the West. By the 1860s, hunting had lost all practical purpose and was just a grisly sport.

Blood Sport

Parties paid handsomely to be taken out onto the prairie for a shoot. Some went on specially chartered trains (right). Carcasses were often left where they fell, or just had the tongues ripped out to be served as a delicacy. One observer measured a stack of buffalo bones 7 feet (2 m) tall stretching for half a mile.

INDIANS AND THE BUFFALO

The traditional lifestyle of the North American Indians depended on the buffalo. The Indians ate buffalo meat and made the hides into clothes, shoes, and tents. Buffalo bone was put to all sorts of uses. It could be carved into weapons and tools, such as needles, or boiled down to make glue.

James Butler Hickok began life as a Kansas farmer. Going west, he quickly gained a reputation as a fast gun. Exaggerating his deeds, Hickok (right) earned the nickname "Wild Bill."

COWBOY MEETS BUFFALO

During the years on either side of the Civil War, many cowboys spent a time as buffalo hunters. They were joined for a while by such famous names as William Cody ("Buffalo Bill"), Bat Masterson, and Wyatt Earp. Buffalo hunting was less arduous than cattle driving, and, for the ordinary cowboy, much more profitable. All a man needed was a steady hand, a powerful rifle, and a plentiful supply of ammunition. Later, when the disastrous consequences of the hunting mania were only too clear, few bragged of what they had done. Buffalo Bill said that he had killed only for food. Cattleman Charles Goodnight regretted ever having taken part in the slaughter.

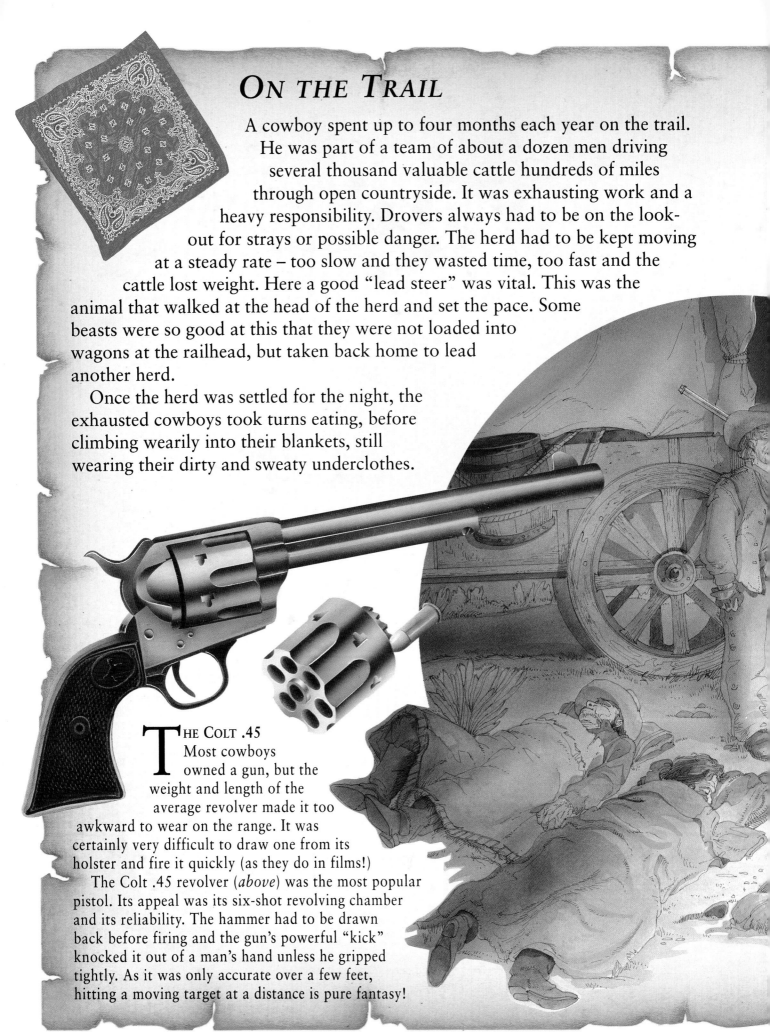

ON THE TRAIL

A cowboy spent up to four months each year on the trail. He was part of a team of about a dozen men driving several thousand valuable cattle hundreds of miles through open countryside. It was exhausting work and a heavy responsibility. Drovers always had to be on the lookout for strays or possible danger. The herd had to be kept moving at a steady rate – too slow and they wasted time, too fast and the cattle lost weight. Here a good "lead steer" was vital. This was the animal that walked at the head of the herd and set the pace. Some beasts were so good at this that they were not loaded into wagons at the railhead, but taken back home to lead another herd.

Once the herd was settled for the night, the exhausted cowboys took turns eating, before climbing wearily into their blankets, still wearing their dirty and sweaty underclothes.

THE COLT .45
Most cowboys owned a gun, but the weight and length of the average revolver made it too awkward to wear on the range. It was certainly very difficult to draw one from its holster and fire it quickly (as they do in films!)

The Colt .45 revolver (*above*) was the most popular pistol. Its appeal was its six-shot revolving chamber and its reliability. The hammer had to be drawn back before firing and the gun's powerful "kick" knocked it out of a man's hand unless he gripped tightly. As it was only accurate over a few feet, hitting a moving target at a distance is pure fantasy!

DANGER!

Although they were excellent horsemen, the greatest danger cowboys faced was being thrown from a horse and dragged along by a foot trapped in the stirrup. There was also the threat of being caught before a stampeding herd or slashed by the horns of an angry steer.

The prairies (*above*) were full of danger. Worst of all was the rattlesnake (*left*), whose bite killed a man within the hour. Wolves, cougars, and pumas were more of a danger to stray cattle, but they might attack a man if cornered. There was a further danger from rustlers and, very occasionally, Indians. Finally, waterbottles (*above right*) had to be kept full to prevent heat exhaustion.

THE KANSAS LINE

I've been where the lightnin', the lightnin' tangled my eyes,
The cattle I could scarcely hold;
Think I heard my boss man say:
"I want all brave-hearted men
who ain't afraid to die
To whoop up the cattle from
morning till night,
Way up on the Kansas Line."

The cowboy's life is a dreadful life,
He's driven through heat and cold;
I'm almost froze with the water on
my clothes,
A-ridin' through heat and cold.

(From *The Kansas Line*, an early cowboy campfire song.)

Nighthawks
Out on the trail, the cowboys never all slept at the same time. Two "nighthawks" (watchmen) stood guard over camp and herd for two-hour shifts.

19

RUM, CARDS, AND WOMEN

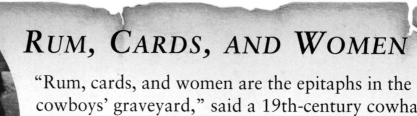

"Rum, cards, and women are the epitaphs in the cowboys' graveyard," said a 19th-century cowhand. What he meant was that when cowboys reached the end of the trail and received their pay, they soon wasted it in a wild spree of entertainment. There was some truth in this. The weeks of cattle driving were hard, dangerous, and dirty. At the end of the ride, as soon as the cattle had been sold, cowboys felt they deserved a little relaxation. But cowboy life in the trail towns was never as exciting as the movies make out, particularly as they earned only $30 a month.

On arrival, they first took a good, long bath (*above*). Then they threw away their clothes and bought new ones. By the time they had taken a room for a few nights, paid for some good grub, a few drinks, and a dance or two in the saloon (*bottom*), and perhaps played a few games of cards, their money was soon gone. Then it was time to climb wearily back into the saddle and head south again in time for the next roundup.

Spittin'

Most cowboys smoked or chewed tobacco. When a wad of 'baccy had lost its flavor, they spat it out into a bowl on the floor, known as a spittoon. Spitting was regarded as bad manners only if you missed the spittoon!

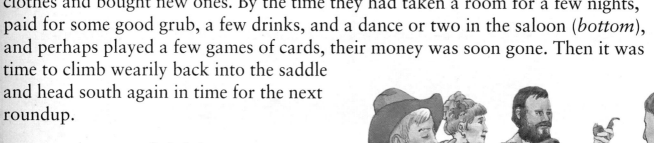

THE SALOON AND THE BAWDY HOUSE

No frontier town was complete without its saloon and bawdy house. The saloon, open all day and night, had a long bar, serving rum, beer, and whiskey in large measures. With beer at 10 cents and whiskey at 12½ cents a glass, many a cowboy ended up with a hangover the next morning. Scattered around were tables and chairs for card players.

The bawdy house, the home of the prairie nymphs, was generally a bit more plush. Here the cowboys could forget the loneliness of the trail with dancing and other intimacies with the prairie nymphs. Nymphs add glamor in the movies (*left*), but for the real-life women, such as Big Nose Kate (*right*), life was often very hard indeed.

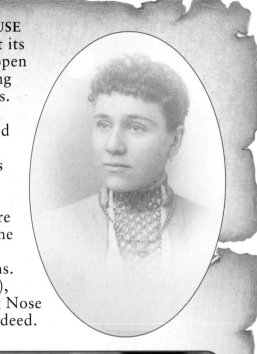

Playing cards (below) *could be a dangerous way to relax. Wild Bill Hickok was shot in the back as he played. Today, his last hand, a combination of aces and eights, is known as a "Dead Man's Hand"!*

QUICK ON THE DRAW. *The saloon doors swing open. The music stops. All eyes turn to the tall stranger. The villain reaches for his revolver – but he is too slow. A single shot rings out and he slumps to the floor. Replacing his .45 in its holster, the gunman nods toward the body on the floor. "I'll have a whiskey... and a coffin for my friend."*

This is the movie saloon. In the real saloons, shooting was uncommon and most bar owners made cowboys take off their guns at the door.

COWGIRLS

Cowboys lived at a time when most women stayed at home caring for children and working around the house. If they went riding, they usually sat sidesaddle. Their long dresses made it hard to rush around and do the same work as men.

In the West, however, things were sometimes rather different. The women who traveled with the wagon trains often worked alongside the men. When they settled, some managed ranches when their menfolk were away, or after they had died. A few even put on men's clothing and joined the drovers on horseback. This caused confusion among the men, who did not know what to make of such "cowgirls." The women they were used to were either nymphs or the mothers and daughters of the homestead. Cowboys therefore regarded cowgirls with a mixture of fear and scorn. One or two women, such as "Cattle Annie" and "Little Britches" (*below*), even joined outlaw gangs. Later, pioneering women worked in rodeo and "Wild West" shows.

CALAMITY JANE

Martha Jane Canary (*above*) was born in Montana in 1852. Her parents died when she was young, forcing her to look after herself. She tried all sorts of jobs, such as cooking and dancing, but found them all rather boring.

In search of excitement, she took to wearing men's clothes and doing men's work. She was a mule driver, railroad laborer and even joined the army, acting as a scout in the Indian Wars.

After that she drifted west, drawing crowds to the saloons with her swashbuckling behavior. Having lived with Wild Bill Hickok for a time, after his death she joined Buffalo Bill's Wild West Show. Sadly, she was now drinking heavily and was soon fired. She spent the rest of her days in drunken poverty. Dying in 1903, she was buried beside Wild Bill.

BELLE STARR

For sheer excitement, few women could match the career of Belle Starr (*left*) known as the "Bandit Queen". Raised as Myra Belle Shirley in a wealthy middle-class home, Belle soon tired of her respectable life and went to live as a bandit.

She shocked people by having two children by men friends and wearing a revolver on a gun belt over her dress. Yet she still rode her horse, *Venus*, side-saddle, like a lady (*right*). She was found guilty of many robberies and had several spells in prison. She married the rustler Sam Starr, and after his death continued to run the ranch as a hideout for outlaws. But one evening, while riding alone, she was killed in an ambush by a fellow bandit.

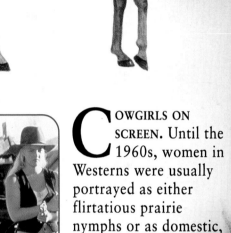

COWGIRLS ON SCREEN. Until the 1960s, women in Westerns were usually portrayed as either flirtatious prairie nymphs or as domestic, pretty and willing to follow their menfolk.

More recent films, such as *Bad Girls* (*left*), have depicted them as tough fighters, but their true role in settling the West is still to be shown.

Cattle Annie And Little Britches

For a time "Oklahoma's Girl Bandits" – Jennie Stevens and Annie McDougal – were the most famous girls in the West. Meeting some of the Doolin gang at a dance, the girls decided to run away from home and join them. Before long, "Cattle" Annie and "Little Britches", as Jennie was known, were robbing with the Doolin gang. But the law was closing in. The girls were finally cornered by Marshal Tilghman and his assistant. Tracking the girls down was one thing – but capturing them was quite another (left). By the time the girls were handcuffed, both men were nursing painful bruises. After two years in prison, Annie married and settled down. Jennie went to New York, where she died of consumption.

LAW AND ORDER

A "cowboy" film nearly always has its gunfight. But true cowboys were not really gunfighters at all. They were cattle drovers. They carried guns for protection against man and beast, but were more likely to use them to shoot a difficult or sick steer than a man.

What the movies have done is mix together two ideas – the lawlessness of the "Wild West" and the life of the cowboy. The only time when cowboys had much to do with lawmen was when they got drunk at the end of a trail and went shouting along the main street (*below*).

During their first few years, most frontier towns were rather wild places. Their law officers, little more than gunmen with a badge, were of two types. One was the elected sheriff and his deputy. The other was the marshal, appointed locally or by the federal (central) government.

On top of a salary of about $100 a month, they could pick up bonuses for each outlaw hanged or shot. The nervous or the fainthearted did not last long in the job.

The Winchester
As well as a revolver, those cowboys who could afford it carried a rifle. The Winchester (above) was the most popular. It weighed 6 pounds (3 kg) and was carried in a holster slung from the saddle. Accurate up to 650 feet (300m), it could be quickly re-loaded using its lever action.

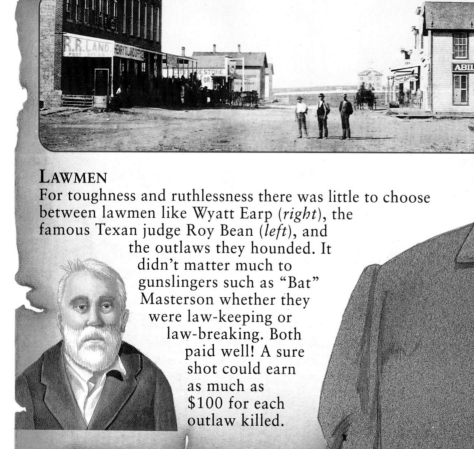

LAWMEN

For toughness and ruthlessness there was little to choose between lawmen like Wyatt Earp (*right*), the famous Texan judge Roy Bean (*left*), and the outlaws they hounded. It didn't matter much to gunslingers such as "Bat" Masterson whether they were law-keeping or law-breaking. Both paid well! A sure shot could earn as much as $100 for each outlaw killed.

The Badge
All lawmen carried a badge of office. The best known was the "tin star" of the sheriff (far right).

The most prestigious badge was the marshal's shield (third on right), which carried the full might of the U.S. government in Washington.

MYTH AT THE OK CORRAL

When silver was found near Tombstone, Arizona, villains flocked there in search of a quick fortune. Among them were Wyatt Earp, his brothers Jim, Morgan, and Virgil, and a sickly killer known as "Doc" Holliday. Virgil was appointed deputy marshal and the Earps began throwing their weight around. This angered the Clanton gang and a showdown was inevitable. Cornering the unarmed Clantons at the OK Corral, the Earps shot them down. Their version of the story caught the popular imagination (*below*), but they were really little more than cold-blooded murderers.

THE POSSE
Outlaws and bandits usually operated in gangs. There was no way a sheriff, even with a deputy, could deal single-handed with several villains on his own.

Therefore, once he knew where the gang was, he had the power to summon a posse (*above*). This was a band of local men willing to act as temporary law officers.

As citizens wanted their town to have a reputation for law and order, there was generally no shortage of eager volunteers.

$5,000.00

REWARD

FOR CAPTURE

DEAD OR ALIVE

OF

BILL DOOLIN

NOTORIOUS ROBBER OF
TRAINS AND BANKS

ABOUT 6 FOOT 2 INCHES TALL, LT. BROWN HAIR,
DANGEROUS, ALWAYS HEAVILY ARMED.

IMMEDIATELY CONTACT THE
U.S. MARSHAL'S OFFICE, GUTHRIE, OKLAHOMA TER.

OUTLAWS

An outlaw is a criminal put beyond the protection of the law. They can be robbed, captured, assaulted, or even killed at will. In the early days of the West, the hard-pressed lawmen found it impossible to bring all villains to justice. As a result, they often resorted to outlawing killers and putting a price on their heads.

"Wanted – Dead or Alive" notices (*left*) were posted all over the state, encouraging people to take the law into their own hands. The great majority of outlaws were common murderers. The outlaw Harry Tacy once declared with cold-blooded frankness, "I kill only those who get in my way."

Nevertheless, there was an air of romance about these rebellious men – and women – living in the wilds outside the law. Some were caught up in the myth of the Wild West and turned into heroes. Even before the age of the movies, 270 novels had been written about the outlaws Jesse and Frank James.

BILLY THE KID

William H. Bonney, "Billy the Kid," was a genuine cowboy outlaw. He committed his first murder at the age of twelve, stabbing a man in a saloon fight. Later, when his ranch boss John Tunstall was killed in a feud, Billy set out on a bloody trail of murder (*right*) and cattle rustling. Before long, he was one of the most wanted men in the West. He was captured twice but managed to get away both times, once when still in irons! Finally, his old enemy Sheriff Pat Garrett tracked Billy down to a house in New Mexico, where he was hiding. The lawmen went in at night. As two men kept him talking on the porch, Garrett shot him dead. Although that was the end of the real Billy the Kid, just twenty-one, the legend had only just begun. The Kid became the subject of books, films, plays, and even a ballet.

Cherokee Bill (left) *killed thirteen men in two years. He was hanged at the age of twenty.*

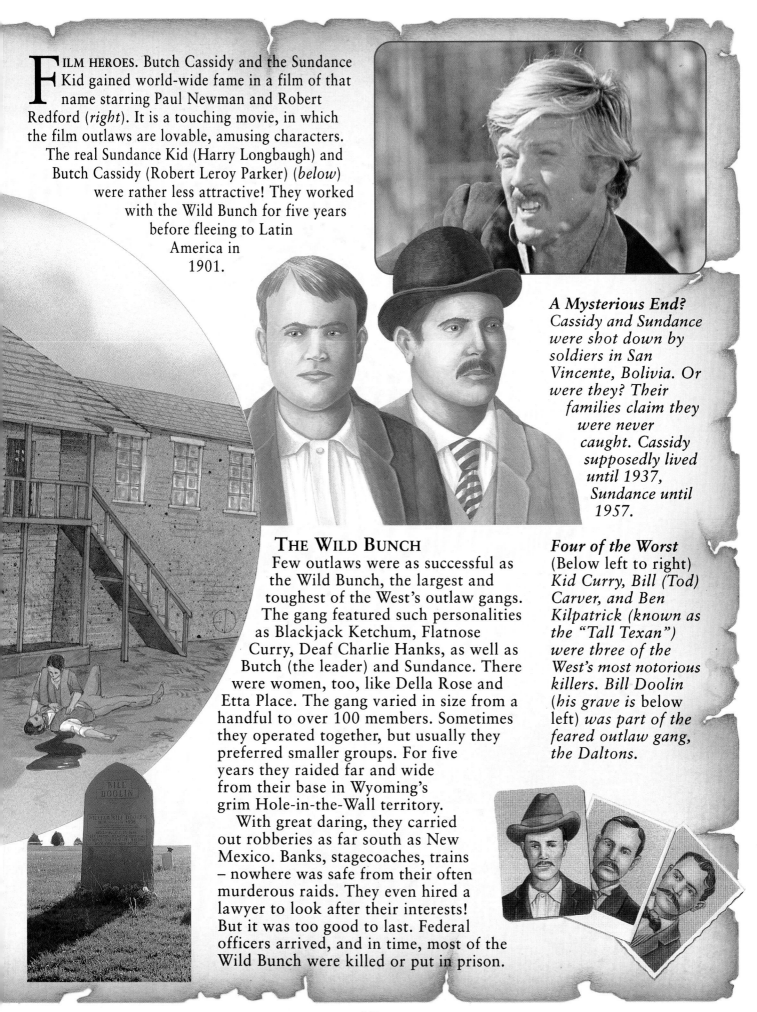

FILM HEROES. Butch Cassidy and the Sundance Kid gained world-wide fame in a film of that name starring Paul Newman and Robert Redford (*right*). It is a touching movie, in which the film outlaws are lovable, amusing characters. The real Sundance Kid (Harry Longbaugh) and Butch Cassidy (Robert Leroy Parker) (*below*) were rather less attractive! They worked with the Wild Bunch for five years before fleeing to Latin America in 1901.

A Mysterious End?
Cassidy and Sundance were shot down by soldiers in San Vincente, Bolivia. Or were they? Their families claim they were never caught. Cassidy supposedly lived until 1937, Sundance until 1957.

THE WILD BUNCH

Few outlaws were as successful as the Wild Bunch, the largest and toughest of the West's outlaw gangs. The gang featured such personalities as Blackjack Ketchum, Flatnose Curry, Deaf Charlie Hanks, as well as Butch (the leader) and Sundance. There were women, too, like Della Rose and Etta Place. The gang varied in size from a handful to over 100 members. Sometimes they operated together, but usually they preferred smaller groups. For five years they raided far and wide from their base in Wyoming's grim Hole-in-the-Wall territory.

With great daring, they carried out robberies as far south as New Mexico. Banks, stagecoaches, trains – nowhere was safe from their often murderous raids. They even hired a lawyer to look after their interests! But it was too good to last. Federal officers arrived, and in time, most of the Wild Bunch were killed or put in prison.

Four of the Worst
(Below left to right) Kid Curry, Bill (Tod) Carver, and Ben Kilpatrick (known as the "Tall Texan") were three of the West's most notorious killers. Bill Doolin (his grave is below left) was part of the feared outlaw gang, the Daltons.

COWBOYS AND INDIANS

Cowboy hostility toward Native Americans – popularly known in the movies as Indians – is another myth of the Wild West. The myth arose because many of the best stories set good against evil, and cowboy films were no exception. The heroes were the cowboys. Searching for villains, film directors and organizers of Wild West shows often selected Indians because their appearance and tactics were good entertainment. The truth was quite different. America's westward expansion was marked by frequent fighting between immigrant and Native Americans, but cowboys were rarely involved.

The Indian Wars that began in 1864 were generally fought between Native groups and the U.S. Army. Real cowboys had little reason to dislike the Indians. In fact, many cowboys *were* Native Americans. Excellent horsemanship, good local knowledge, and the ability to survive in tough conditions made them ideal cattlemen. No drover taking cattle through Indian territory wanted to make his difficult job still harder by stirring up trouble with the local people.

CUSTER'S LAST STAND

No Native group resented the arrival of the White Man into its territory more than the Sioux. Things came to a head in 1874, when gold was discovered on Sioux territory in Dakota. Miners came in the thousands, ignoring the rights of the locals. The Sioux attacked, destroying the settlers' camps. One of the U.S. army officers given the task of settling the disturbance was Colonel George Armstrong Custer. On June 25, 1876, Custer led his troop of 215 men right into a Sioux ambush. They were wiped out in under an hour (*above*).

WHITEWASH. Another cowboy myth is that all cattlemen were descended from white Europeans. Mexicans and Native and African Americans all joined the cowboy ranks, and the cowboy language was not English but Spanish.

Almost one in seven cowboys was black. Nat Love, for example, won many rodeo competitions for his skill with the rope and revolver. John Ware, another African American cowboy, had the reputation of being the best bronco tamer in the West.

Indian Territory
Anyone taking cattle across an Indian reservation had to pay them a dollar per head of cattle. The trail boss often employed Native Americans (left) to negotiate the fee.

Friendly Trade
Real-life cowboys much preferred talking with Native Americans to fighting them. While on the trail, they often depended on Indian traders for fresh food and other essential supplies (above).

THE LONE RANGER was one of the most popular TV cowboys of the 1950s. The masked figure on a white horse helped folk in their fight against lawlessness. He was accompanied by an Indian, Tonto. The white hero and his loyal Native American servant was typical of the way Hollywood depicted the Native Americans. It helped perpetuate the lie of white supremacy so resented by non-white Americans.

THE STAGECOACH

In hundreds of cowboy films, "stages" are held up by outlaws or chased by whooping Indians across broad landscapes of cactus and rocky outcrops. In reality, the stagecoach had little to do with the life of a cowboy.

Before the railroad, the coach was the principal means of passenger transportation. The name "stagecoach" came from the practice of making long journeys in several stages, changing horses at each stopping place. This reduced travel time and kept the horses fresh.

Along the poor roads of the West, a coach traveled for up to fifteen hours a day, covering 40-60 miles (60-100 km) in the summer and perhaps half that in the winter.

A large coach might carry fourteen passengers. The more expensive seats were on the inside, sheltered from the sun, dust, and rain. Others made do with seats on the roof. The coach carried an armed guard, known as the "shotgun" from the weapon he carried. He usually sat next to the driver.

S TAGECOACH. The film that first gave the stagecoach a central role in the Western movie was John Ford's classic black and white movie, *Stagecoach* (*above*). Starring John Wayne, it used the simple idea of a coach journey to examine the relationship between passengers who experience every kind of adventure, from hold-up to an attack by Indians. Many film directors have copied Ford's ideas and techniques, but not one has bettered them.

An Eccentric Robber
Charles E. Bolton, known as "Black Bart," prided himself on never spilling a drop of blood and robbing only coach companies. He was distinguished by his educated accent, the sack he wore over his head (cut with two eye holes), and poetry he left in the boxes he had robbed!

PONY EXPRESS

This was a rapid mail service. Using 80 riders and 500 horses, it operated in a relay between 190 stations.

At each station a rider (*left*) had two minutes to transfer himself and his mail bags to a fresh mount.

In 1860 the first mail was carried and cost $5 to carry a letter the 1,980 miles (3,168 km) from St. Joseph, Missouri to Sacramento, California.

Gee Up!
Stagecoaches were pulled by a team of four or eight horses, depending on the size of the coach or the nature of the terrain.

Pearl Hart
The West's last stage robbery was committed by Joe Boot and schoolgirl Pearl Hart (below left). Holding up a stage in Arizona, they took $431 dollars from three passengers – then got lost!

After wandering in the cold and rain for three days, they fell asleep. They were awakened by the local sheriff.

Pearl was given five years in jail, but was let out early.

STICK 'EM UP!

In the sparsely-populated West, stages made tempting targets for bandits. Passengers often carried money, and coaches transported mail and other valuables. In 1877 the Wells Fargo company was robbed 200 times in a month!

Masked robbers liked to ambush a coach midway between two staging posts. While one or more robbers covered the guard and passengers in case they tried to fight, the others halted the stage. The guard was told to throw down his gun and any boxes he was carrying. The passengers were then forced to hand over their valuables.

THE RAILROAD

The railroad was the making and the breaking of the cowboy. His principal job was to round up cattle and drive them to the nearest railroad station. Without railroads, the cattle boom could never have taken place.

But as the rail network expanded, so the length of the cattle trail shrank. By the 1890s, cowboys only had to take their herds a few miles to the nearest slaughterhouse, where they were killed and loaded onto wagons bound for the North and East.

In 1861, the United States had only about 30,000 miles (50,000 km) of railroad, all in the East. In 1864, the Union Pacific Railroad began a transcontinental line. This joined up with the Central Pacific Railroad in 1869. By 1900, the United States had 200,000 miles of track.

OVER MOUNTAIN AND RIVER

Because a locomotive hauling heavy wagons or passenger cars was unable to climb a steep gradient, the tracks had to be laid on comparatively level ground.

To achieve this, hillsides were blasted away and huge bridges were constructed across rivers and valleys (*below*). Not surprisingly, some of the work was shoddy and there were terrible accidents.

RAILROAD LABORERS

The first transcontinental line was built largely by the labor of recent immigrants. The Central Pacific used Chinese workers and the Union Pacific Irish laborers (*above right*).

The work was incredibly tough, particularly in the winter, but it was not well paid. In addition to the many accidents, workers were attacked by wild animals and Native Americans. In the end, workers and directors cheered with delight when the two lines met at Promontory Point in Utah.

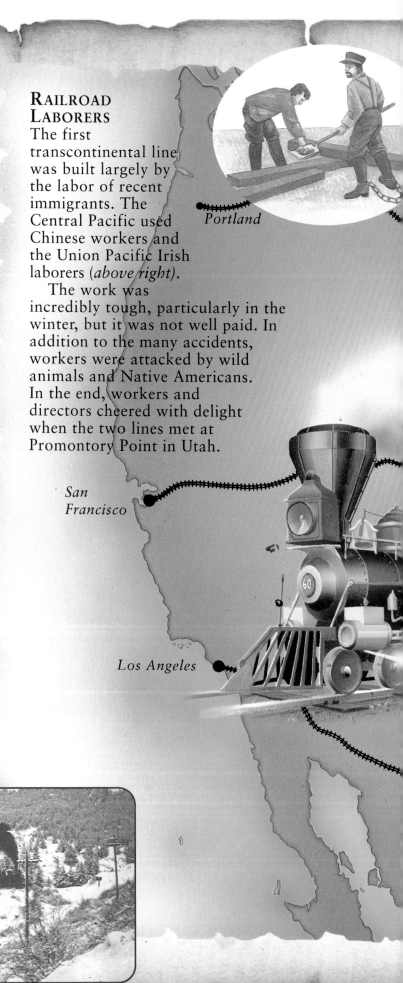

Portland

San Francisco

Los Angeles

Settlers were never far behind the railroad. In 1862, Congress passed a Homestead Act. This entitled settlers to a 160-acre farm, on payment of a $10 fee, if they had lived on a piece of land for five years. The West was soon dotted with homesteads.

Bismarck

Miles City

RAILROAD WEALTH

The government gave the Union Pacific a set amount of land for each section of track it laid. The company gained about 20 million acres (8 million hectares) of land, making its directors very rich men.

Minneapolis

Chicago

Laramie

Cheyenne

Ogallata

Omaha

St. Joseph

Denver

Dodge City

Abilene

Kansas City

Sedalia

St. Louis

Newton

Robbing trains was even more tempting than robbing stages. But it took a well-organized group such as the one led by Jesse James (below) to pull off a successful robbery.

A GROWING NETWORK

Other rail routes soon followed the transcontinental line – the Southern Pacific line ran from San Francisco to New Orleans. In time a line was built from El Paso to Kansas City, and the days of the long drive were numbered.

Dennison

El Paso

Houston

San Antonio

BACK AT THE RANCH

By 1895 the Cattle Kingdom was over. The long drive was gone and the open prairie was being parceled into farms. The ranch had always been at the heart of the cattle business. Originally it consisted of the boss's house, a bunkhouse, outbuildings, and a corral for the horses. By the 20th century it included barns for cattle in winter and was surrounded by fenced fields. There are several reasons for the decline of the traditional cowboy way of life. One was the advance of the railway and the increasing number of homesteaders (nicknamed "sodbusters") and their wired-off fields. By the 1880s, there were simply more cattle than people wanted to buy. Sheep (*above*) became more profitable, and sheepherders and cattlemen fought over grazing.

The cattle boom was also hit by "Texas fever." This disease spread rapidly and Kansas closed its borders to cattle from the South. Finally, the severe winter of 1886–1887 killed half the cattle on the northern ranges.

water pump →

ranchhouse

bunkhouse

BARBED WIRE

Barbed wire (*above*) was first manufactured by Joseph F. Glidden in 1874. To begin with he turned out just a few hundred yards a week. The demand was so huge, however, that by 1883 his American Steel & Wire Co. was producing over 600 miles (950 km) a day.

Barbed wire enabled a farmer to erect a cattle-proof fence in hours, dividing up the range and making it impossible for cattle to move freely over their traditional grazing lands.

MAIL ORDER

Most ranches and homesteads were a long way from the nearest store, and even then it only stocked the bare necessities.

To cater for other requirements, enterprising salesmen developed the mail order business, displaying their wares in glossy catalogs, called "wish books."

THE BUNKHOUSE

When on the ranch, cowboys lived and ate in a bunkhouse. With ten men to a low, wooden building, they had few comforts.

Language was bad, the air was stale, and the accommodation was sparse. The house was cold in the winter and stifling hot in the summer, with little privacy. Most cowboys were pleased to get out on the trail again!

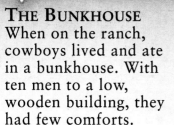

Winter nights were spent in the bunkhouse. Cowboys played games, braided rope (above), or sat talking and smoking, waiting for the spring.

O KLAHOMA! The clash between cowboy and farmer is one of the themes in the musical *Oklahoma!* (1943, *below*). One of its songs suggests that "the farmer and the cowman should be friends." In real life this was rarely the case. Ranchers had always grazed cattle on the open prairie. When homesteaders began fencing in land, claiming it their own, the cowboys were angry but powerless to stop them.

barn

Cruel winters *could ruin a rancher in the northern states. Cattle often froze or got buried in blizzards.*

SETTLIN' DOWN

Cowboys were young, rarely over thirty (*right*). Life in the saddle was tough, and many suffered broken bones and premature aging. Few men endured the hardships for more than ten years.

Many cowboys dreamed of the day when they would have enough money to have a ranch of their own.

COWBOYS OF THE WORLD

American cowboys were only one of many groups of famous herdsmen who relied on horses for their work. They are the best known, not because they were any more skilled than other riders, but because their way of life has been made famous by hundreds of novels and films. Humans first learned to tame and ride the horse thousands of years ago. The invention of the stirrup in the 4th century AD gave riders extra control of their mounts. Until the widespread use of tractors in the mid-20th century, the horse was the indispensable friend of farmers around the globe.

Cowboys and mounted shepherds were found where animals grazed on wide open pastures, such as the Australian Outback or the Hungarian Plain. And cowboys can still be seen today on some of the more remote grazing lands.

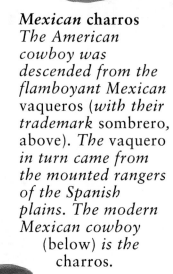

Mexican charros
The American cowboy was descended from the flamboyant Mexican vaqueros (*with their trademark* sombrero, above). *The* vaquero *in turn came from the mounted rangers of the Spanish plains. The modern Mexican cowboy* (below) *is the* charros.

***The South American* gaucho** (below *and* right) *was a cattle herder working on the broad* pampas *of Argentina and Uruguay. They were famous for catching cattle with the* bolas, *a short rope or chain with weights at either end.*

N ED KELLY, the son of an Irish convict transported to Australia by the British, was the most famous Australian cowboy outlaw. In 1878 he wounded a policeman trying to arrest his brother. Fleeing the law, the Kelly brothers formed an outlaw gang.

They settled on the border between Victoria and New South Wales, where they made several daring robberies before being tracked down and captured. Ned was hanged in Melbourne at the age of twenty-five. However, like many young American outlaws, he became a folk hero, and numerous stories – usually untrue – grew up around him.

Hungarian csikosok
Hungarians are descended from the Magyars, daring horsemen who swept into Eastern Europe in the 9th century. The csikosok *cowboy (third from left) of the Hungarian Plain keeps alive his ancestors' tradition of brilliant horsemanship.*

Camargue gardian
For centuries horsemen have roamed the Camargue, the marshy area at the mouth of the Rhone River in France, famous for horse and cattle breeding. Today, mounted gardians (below) can still be found there.

Australian stockman
Although four-wheel-drive vehicles now churn across the Australian outback, some stockmen still prefer to round up their cattle on horseback (first horseman on right).

Like America, Australia had no cattle until they were introduced by settlers in the 19th century.

Australian cowboys at a school for cattlemen (above). They are wearing "Drizabones," a waxed coat, popular with cowboys, whose name says it all!

BUFFALO BILL

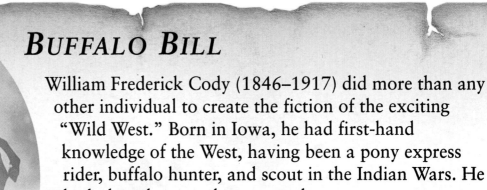

William Frederick Cody (1846–1917) did more than any other individual to create the fiction of the exciting "Wild West." Born in Iowa, he had first-hand knowledge of the West, having been a pony express rider, buffalo hunter, and scout in the Indian Wars. He had, though, never been a cowboy.

He didn't let this worry him, and when he noticed a growing public interest in the American West in the early 1880s, "Buffalo Bill" decided to cash in. In 1883 he organized Buffalo Bill's Wild West Show (*below*).

The three-hour entertainment was largely myth, but it was what the audiences wanted, and all over America and Europe they flocked to see it. Cowboys and Indians, dressed in spotless costume, enacted battles and hold-ups. Artists gave daring demonstrations of riding, roping, and marksmanship.

Real life stars were taken on, such as Sitting Bull, Calamity Jane, and the sureshot Annie Oakley. The show eventually lost popularity to the movies, and Bill died heavily in debt. But by then the myth of the Wild West was established.

BUFFALO BILL'S INDIANS

Buffalo Bill had fought against the Indians and had great admiration for their courage and skills. But his show demanded colorful villains to set off against his mythical cowboys. Indians fitted the bill perfectly.

However, the image of them that was burned into the audience's mind did the Native American peoples a great injustice.

Dime Novels
In the early 20th century, thousands of simple adventure stories featured the reinvented cowboy, no longer a cattleman but a noble fighter.

BUCK TAYLOR
William Levi "Buck" Taylor (*right*) was the star of the Wild West Show. A real Texas cowboy who worked at Cody's ranch, he was a fine horseman who knew a trick or two with the rope.

Buck set the trend for "authentic" cowboy dress – the Stetson, spurs, checkered shirt, bright neckerchief, jeans, and elaborately tooled boots.

Nice Shooting!
Annie Oakley could slice a card in two with a single bullet. Even more amazing was her ability to shoot through the pips of cards thrown into the air (left). Her life was turned into the musical Annie Get Your Gun.

MISSIE MAKES A HIT
Phoebe Ann Oakley Mozee was born in Ohio in 1860. At fifteen she won her first major shooting contest, and in 1886 she entered Buffalo Bill's Wild West Show as "Little Missie" or "The Peerless Wing and Rifle Shot." Annie was the darling of audiences the world over. She shot cigarettes from her husband's mouth and coins from between his fingers. One trick involved releasing two clay pigeons, leaping on a table, picking up a gun, and shooting them before they hit the ground!

THE WESTERN

More Westerns have been made in Hollywood than any other type of film. The early filmmakers took their ideas straight from the Wild West shows and dime novels of the time. The Wild West was an obvious choice of subject. It was already immensely popular. It also offered beautiful surroundings close to the film studios in California, and ready-made and identifiable heroes (the cowboys) and villains (the Indians and outlaws).

Early film directors continued and exaggerated all the old inaccuracies. Women were only included in films to add romantic interest and so that brave cowboys could rescue them from terrible fates. Native Americans were either ridiculous or wholly evil. African Americans hardly featured at all. If they did, it was as servants. Mexicans were invariably silly or pathetic, or both. Only in the 1960s did this formula begin to change. But the true world of the cowboy has yet to be shown on film as it really was.

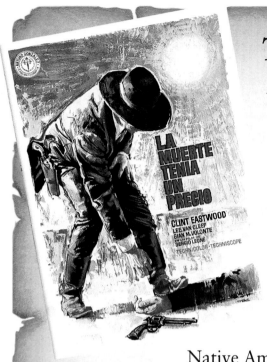

WESTERNS OLD AND NEW

Westerns tend to reflect the age in which they were made. In the 1920s and 1930s, cowboys were clean-cut, honest fighters against evil (such as Tom Mix, *first on right*). During the 1930s, when America was hit by economic depression, musicals offered escape from reality. This gave rise to "singing cowboys" like Gene Autry (*second on right*), who strummed away on his guitar beside the campfire.

During the 1950s John Wayne (*third on right*) introduced yet another type of cowboy – the rock-hard moralist. In a less certain age, Clint Eastwood (*far right*) portrayed anarchist cowboys. Today, Westerns attempt to re-discover the role of women, Native and African Americans in the making of the West.

COMIC COWBOYS. As part of the "Western mania" that swept the world in the first half of the 20th century, cowboys found their way into children's comic books. These took two forms. One echoed the cowboys of the movies. A typical hero of this type was Jeff Arnold of the British *Eagle*. Jeff was strong, silent, and duty-bound to see right prevail. The other type was the comedian, such as the massively strong Desperate Dan. France, too, had its comic cowboys. One was Lucky Luke (*left*), "the man who could draw faster than his shadow!"

Cowboy Classics
Many regard High Noon *as the best cowboy movie ever (below). The story is simple – a sheriff waits for the return on the noon train of villains he had sent to jail. But the acting and atmosphere combine to produce a great film.*

(Above) *The return of the screen cowboy* – The Unforgiven.

JOHN WAYNE
Who would go to see a Western starring Marion Morrison? Not many, which was why he changed his name to John Wayne and became the most successful cowboy actor Hollywood ever produced. In 1939 Wayne made his name playing the Ringo Kid in *Stagecoach*. He then went on to star in over 80 films.

THE RODEO

The rodeo began when cowboys pitted their skills against each other in the corral. As the idea of the Wild West grew in popularity, so rodeos became more organized. Shows were held outside the Old West, audiences paid to watch and large prizes were awarded. Rodeos still draw huge crowds all over North America (*above*). Many competitors are professional, traveling from rodeo to rodeo. Country and Western music is played and traditional cowboy food is served. But the high point is always the competition, which includes bronco riding, calf roping, steer wrestling and, most dangerous of all, bull riding.

Roping
In trying to lasso a young steer as it careens wildly around the arena, the cowboy relies on his horse as much as his own skill. After he has caught the animal, he has to throw it to the ground and tie its legs with a knot that holds for at least six seconds.

BAREBACK BRONCO RIDING
Small, lively horses are specially bred for this event. The rider mounts in a pen outside the arena. As soon as the gate is opened, the horse charges into the open, bucking wildly.

The rider has to stay on for only a few seconds. If that sounds easy – just try it! The rider faces the danger of being thrown off and being crushed against the side of the pen.

Saddled bronco riding is easier than bareback riding, so to make it tougher, riders are allowed to hold on with only one hand. The same saddle is used by all competition riders.

42

RODEO STARS

A man or woman can make a fair living from rodeo work. But it's a tough life. Professional competitors (*right*) travel around the country, taking part in perhaps 100 shows a year. They pay an entry fee and receive no reward unless they win a prize. Every rodeo has its fair share of broken bones, and there is always the dreaded possibility of being gored or trampled by a bull.

A Rodeo belt buckle (left).

Steer wrestling (known as bulldoggin') arose out of the need for cowboys to haul calves to the ground for branding. In the rodeo it is done against the clock. African American cowboy Bill Pickett (1860–1932) is said to have bitten the cow's lip to force it down (right).

Rodeo clowns (right) *enlivened rodeos from the earliest days. They attempted the same events as the cowboy but with deliberate incompetence. Although amusing to watch, clowning is very dangerous. Their short pants are actually an aid to safety.*

WORLDWIDE SKILLS

The Rodeo is a North American show, but it is sometimes held elsewhere in the world (*below*). Other countries have different tests of horsemanship. The most international events are those contested in the Olympic Games – show jumping, dressage, and cross-country riding.

RIDE 'EM, COWBOY!

The interest in cowboys is as strong today as it has ever been. It is not that people want to be cowboys, or even that they know what the life of the cowboy was really like. The cowboy is no longer a historical fact, but a legend and a symbol. He stands for qualities people believe are missing from their lives. To Americans, and all those influenced by the American way of life, he represents the qualities that "made America great" – individualism, enterprise, toughness, honor, and strength. The cowboy also stands for the "natural" life.

The more people live in polluted cities, dependent on the car and electric light, the more they hanker after a way of life that is gone. They dream of the simple existence, of wide open spaces, and sleeping beneath the stars. As the future looks ever more uncertain, they seek reassurance in the past. And for millions, that past is represented by a strong, solitary figure on horseback – the cowboy.

SOAP COWBOYS. During the 1980s, the cowboy image was boosted by the immensely popular TV soap opera, *Dallas* (*below*). Set in Texas, it featured J.R. Ewing, the man you loved to hate. J.R. was an oilman, not a cowboy. But his roots were firmly in the ways of the Wild West. J.R. was not very honest, but he was hard, determined, and plain-spoken. He lived on a ranch and wore a Stetson and cowboy boots. The message to viewers was clear – success in the modern world must be based on foundations laid the previous century by that most American of Americans, the cowboy of the Wild West.

Man of action, the 12-inch (30-cm) cowboy (right)!

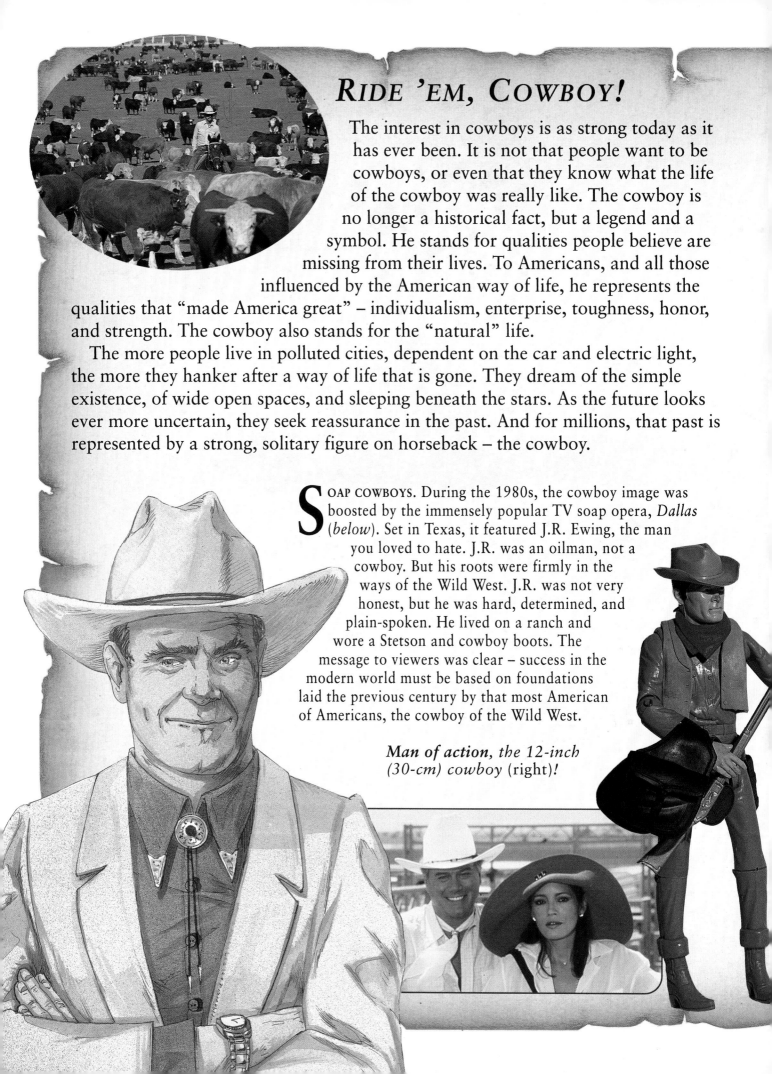

THE COWBOY PRESIDENT

Ronald Wilson Reagan, the 40th president of the United States, understood the power of the legendary cowboy better than most. Before becoming a politician, he had acted in several cowboy films (*left*).

In the late 1970s, the American people had been defeated in Vietnam, the economy was in a slump, President Richard Nixon resigned in disgrace, and crime was rising. In other words, the going was tough. And in American folklore, when the going gets tough, it is time to send for the cowboy.

Reagan promoted himself as that savior cowboy. He wore cowboy clothes and cultivated a strong, no-nonsense image... getting himself elected president, twice!

The cowboy image has been used by advertisers to sell all kinds of products, from clothing to cigarettes. Wares are said to be "authentic," even though real cowboys would have never seen them.

BUSINESS AND GUNS

The idea of the cowboy has spread around the world (*above*). But in the United States it lives on in many forms. One is dress. It is not uncommon for people in some states to go to work dressed in suits and neckties – rounded off with a Stetson and cowboy boots! As one oil magnate said, "My boots are my roots!"

Also, despite the thousands of armed robberies and shootings every year, all attempts to deprive U.S. citizens of their weapons have failed. Deep in their hearts, many Americans are still cowboys.

Jeans (right) *began life as canvas pants for miners. They were later reinforced with patent copper studs, and denim was used instead of canvas.*

THE LANGUAGE OF THE WILD WEST

.45 The Colt .45 revolver.

Bandanna Cheap scarf printed with a bright red dye.

Beeves Cowboy slang for cattle; plural of beef.

Bronco An untrained horse, from the Spanish word for "wild."

Buckaroo A Texan cowboy, a mispronunciation of the Mexican word *vaquero*.

Buffalo Another name for the North American bison.

Bunkhouse A cowboy's communal home on the ranch.

Cattle Kingdom The period when beef production was at its height, roughly 1866–1886.

Cinch A wide strap used to hold the saddle on a horse.

Chaps Leggings worn by cowboys (*above*).

Chuck Cowboy slang for food.

Corral Fenced area for horses, cattle, and other animals.

Cutting horse A horse specially trained to cut (separate) unbranded calves from their mothers.

Federal Of the United States government.

Fenders Leather flaps on the side of the saddle that protect the rider's legs from the horse's sweat.

Great Plains The level plains of the central United States.

Hair pants Goat-hair chaps worn during winter to keep warm.

Hollywood The center of the U.S. film industry, based in Los Angeles.

Indians Native Americans.

Jinglebobs Attachment to a spur that creates a noise when a cowboy walks around.

Lariat or lasso A cowboy's rope.

Long drive Taking cattle north to the railroad.

Longhorn A breed of cow popular in the West.

Long johns One-piece underwear worn by cowboys.

Maverick A wild cow or bull.

Mustang A wild horse.

Nighthawk A camp watchman and guard.

Nymph Cowboy slang for a girl or woman.

Outlaw A criminal denied the protection of the law.

Pioneer One of the early settlers in the West.

Quarter horse Horse bred for its speed over short distances.

Railhead The place where railroad tracks stopped.

Ranch A livestock farm.

Remuda Herd of spare horses.

Revolver A pistol holding several shots in a revolving chamber.

Rodeo A competition of cowboy skills.

Rustler A thief, usually of cattle.

Saloon A bar.

Sodbusters Another name for homesteaders.

Stampede Horses and cattle scattering and running after a sudden fright.

Steer A male calf raised for beef (*above*).

Stetson A famous type of cowboy hat.

Stirrup A foot rest, usually a loop of iron hanging from the saddle (*far left*).

Vaqueros Mexican cowboys, the original cattlemen of the West.

Western A cowboy film.

Winchester A famous make of rifle.

Wrangler The cowboy who looked after the horses in the *remuda*. He was usually a young man learning the trade.

COWBOY TIMELINE

1493 Columbus brings cattle to America on his second voyage.

1500s Cattle introduced into Mexico by the Spanish.

1700s Spanish cattle make their way into Texas. About 100 million buffalo roam the Great Plains at this time.

1800s Spanish methods of handling cattle on horseback enter the American colonies. Frontiersmen who had moved to the American West become cowboys.

1836 Texas declares its independence from Mexico, but many *vaqueros* stay on.

1844 Texas joins the United States.

1850–1880 20 million bison killed by hunters.

1860s The first appearance of the cowboy boot!

1860 First mail sent by Pony Express.

1862 Homestead Act passed by Congress to encourage settlers to move to the West.

1863 Abolition of slavery. Some 200,000 African Americans fight for the North.

1864 Start of Indian Wars.

1865 End of the American Civil War signals beginning of great cattle raising era. Many ex-soldiers sign up as cowboys.

1866 Cowboys drive thousands of cattle to the railroad station in Sedalia, Missouri, in the first major trail drive. However, a few angry farmers with shotguns persuade ranchers to find another route!

1867 Union Pacific Railroad reaches Abilene, Kansas, which was west of the farm belt. Chisholm Trail opens. It runs 1,000 miles (1,600 km) from southern Texas to Abilene.

1869 Union Pacific Railroad and Central Pacific Railroad meet in Utah.

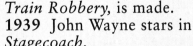

1870 Ranchers discover that cattle could survive cold winters in the northern Plains. Ranches spring up in region of modern Montana, Wyoming, Colorado, and the Dakotas. Cowboys move north with cattle.

1870s Ranchers begin experimenting with European breeds such as the Hereford.

1874 Joseph Glidden starts manufacturing barbed wire.

1876 Western Trail opens, after farmers settle beyond Abilene. Abilene and Dodge City boom as cattle towns. Sioux ambush Custer at Little Big Horn. Wild Bill Hickok is shot in the back playing poker.

1881 Gustavus Swift invents the refrigerated meat wagon. Billy the Kid is shot by Pat Garrett.

1883 Buffalo Bill organizes the first Wild West Show.

1885 Almost 50 per cent of land in the United States is used for cattle raising.

1886–87 Severe winters kill half the cattle on the northern ranges.

1886 End of the Cattle Kingdom.

1889 Belle Star ambushed and killed.

1903 The first cowboy film, *The Great Train Robbery*, is made.

1939 John Wayne stars in *Stagecoach*.

1952 Gary Cooper stars in *High Noon*.

1965 National Cowboy Hall of Fame opens in Oklahoma City.

INDEX

Photographic credits *Abbreviations: t – top, m – middle, b – bottom, l – left.* Front & back cover top, 9t, 30b – United Artists (courtesy Kobal). Front cover bottom, 25m – Universal (courtesy Kobal). 6t, 8-9, 10b, 11, 15, 17 all, 20b, 21tr, 23t, 24, 28m, 32, 33b, 39tl, 47 all – Denver Library, Western History Department. 6m – 20th Century Fox (courtesy Kobal). 7, 37t, 38m, 39tr – Hulton Deutsch. 10t, 12, 13t & ml, 14, 16, 19b, 21m, 22, 23m, 26t, 27 all, 30t, 33t, 34t, 36 all, 37b, 38t, 41t, 42, 43 all, 44t & bl, 45 tr inset, 45mr, 46 all – Frank Spooner Pictures. 13m, 20t, 40, 41b – Ronald Grant Archive. 18, 19t, 35b, 44br – Roger Vlitos. 21t, 25t, 28t, 34b, 38-39 – Range Pictures/Bettmann Archive. 25b – Paramount Pictures (courtesy Kobal). 26b, 29m – Western History Collections, University of Oklahoma Library. 29b – Kobal Collection. 35t – Magna Theatre (courtesy Kobal). 41m – Stanley Kramer/United Artists (courtesy Kobal). 45tl – RKO (courtesy Kobal). 45ml – By kind permission of Levis Strauss & Co Commercial "Campfire" with special thanks to photographer Ely Pouget, actor Ethan Brown & Prima management.